The Daily P[...]
Companion Jour[...]

a creative notebook to be used in conjunction with
The Daily Poet: Day-By-Day Prompts For Your Writing Practice

Two Sylvias Press

Two Sylvias Press
PO Box 1524
Kingston, WA 98346
twosylviaspress@gmail.com

Cover Design: Kelli Russell Agodon
Book Design: Annette Spaulding-Convy

Created with the belief that *great writing is good for the world*, Two Sylvias Press mixes modern technology, classic style, and literary intellect with an eco-friendly heart. We draw our inspiration from the poetic literary talent of Sylvia Plath and the editorial business sense of Sylvia Beach. We are an independent press dedicated to publishing the exceptional voices of writers.

For more information about Two Sylvias Press please visit: www.twosylviaspress.com

ISBN-13: 978-0692450895

ISBN-10: 0692450890

Two Sylvias Press
www.twosylviaspress.com

Introduction

Not the storm cloud, low-hanging in anticipation, you are the precipitation
—your ink to this page, the release awaited.
  ~ Natasha Moni, author of *The Cardiologist's Daughter*

Dear Poet:

Your poems are waiting to be released on these pages.

In 2013, Kelli Russell Agodon and Martha Silano created *The Daily Poet: Day-By-Day Prompts For Your Writing Practice* to help spark creativity in your writing for each of the 365 days in a year. However, after publishing this book, Two Sylvias Press has had many requests to create a journal companion to use **with** *The Daily Poet*. This journal is a response to that request.

We understand that writing a poem-a-day can become a practice—a meditation even—and poets have found themselves writing poems with what William Stafford called "the golden thread," an image originally from a William Blake poem. This *golden thread* is an idea or theme that moves throughout your work. Perhaps there is an image or theme you find reappearing in your poems. Our hope is that *The Daily Poet Companion Journal*—if used every day (or *almost* every day)—will create a way for you to return to your work all at once, reread your poems at a later time so that you can see what weaves them together.

We believe in the importance of pen to paper. In a world where we wake up, check our smartphones, type emails to family members, *The Daily Poet Companion Journal* is a way to take us back to the basics. Many times our creativity is linked to the muscle memory of holding a pen, writing a word, drawing a picture. Let yourself doodle on the page as you write—something you can't do in a computer document— and allow your mind to wander.

This journal wants to become your good habit of writing daily. Most manuscripts contain 48 poems—if 25% of your daily poems work out, you will have 93 new poems at the end of the year. If only 15% work out, you will still have enough poems for a full-length manuscript. Consider this journal a step towards your poetic future, a few more poems to send out into the world.

Poet January Gill O'Neil says, *If don't write every day, then you put pressure on yourself to write the perfect draft every time you sit down. Write often, at any time during the day or night, whenever the mood strikes you. No excuses. Give yourself a chance to be imperfect and to fail—that's when the magic happens. The Daily Poet Companion Journal* is a place to hold your perfect imperfections.

Think of this journal as a safe place to exercise your brain, your word play, your literary imagination. It will become a poem diary of your year, capturing what you've been inspired to write. It's okay if you miss a day, as the *The Daily Poet Companion Journal* will keep a clear record of each exercise you have completed or skipped. The goal of this journal is to encourage your writing practice by organizing the poems that you have created from *The Daily Poet* prompts. Use it however you like—it's *your* journal.

We've included space for you to write down your monthly goals, your notes for future poems, and any creative ideas or doodles. Some days you may not be able to write a poem, so you might want to jot down a list of images or phrases. You may find yourself writing down snippets of conversation you overhear, childhood memories, or inspirational lines from your favorite poets. It's all good. We want to bring more writing into your life, and we hope *The Daily Poet Companion Journal* gives you a space to do just that.

Now, write on . . .

Art enables us to find ourselves and lose ourselves at the same time. ~Thomas Merton

JANUARY

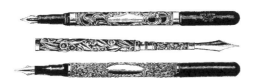

Goals/Notes/Doodles:

JANUARY

1

. . . .

New Year's Resolutions

Be the kindest you have ever been

Sit under a tree, at least once a week

Have a 'phone a loved one' day

Begin again, every day

Stay active and in great shape

Write. Write. Write. Even when doubt comes to play.

Believe in yourself and believe in humanity

Spread love and laugh when you can

Be still and grateful, God has a plan.

Keep your room tidy and full of life

Be the light in everyones life

Read books and study quran

Listen to meditation everyday

Smile. Always.

Always begin with Ya Allah ♡

JANUARY

2

. . . .

Protecting Niagara Falls

Protect the way my heart wept
Oh Allah, protect the soul that stretches and doesn't know where
to go yet. Give it love with seeds, so it can grow whether the sky
be dry or wet. If I do not have this yearnership for you, whom will
I beg? If you run to me, may I catch. May I learn to savour the
solace of your mercy. Oh rahman, you are to me as nothing else
is.

Let me write this contract as contradiction for what my soul tends
to.

Let it be that I am only to weep for you.

I am needy and nothing holds my soul quite like you do.

JANUARY

3

....

Censored

Sex

Intimacy

haram

hiding

Rape

Righteousness

Rose

Rebirth

I'm not sure what words I haven't wrote before

they all seem so new to me now anyway

with a shift in perspective, comes a greater wall of vocabulary

knowing we use them

Understand their hearts

like needy children

I am in need of great love

yet I know this famished heart is in need of growth

will I die to myself

enough to use new words

words that bleed into shame and shyness

Censored like a pilgrim is to his hopes

JANUARY

4

....

I Hear It's Cold In Antarctica

distance	ice cubes	wooden creak
darkness	finger tips	door knob
motorway	nails	heartbeat
Rain	tips	
Emptiness	toes	
Cold bed	skin	
water	piano keys	

In the rain she prays again for it to drench her scent
as the highways of the motorway mirror her moments of regret
her escape and scent belong in a cold bed
stormy weather and faces left undone
haven't been able to tune myself
true piano keys undreamt of

unheard of
undealt with. This is a poem about a season where there ought
to be movement. Miracles. A door knob turns and it is colder in
another room. Summer blooms away as it blooms. Living in the
heat like a lamp. Longing and trying for a length of time without
the emptiness. It's been weeks and months, nearly a year.

JANUARY

5

....

Vision Persona

She prepares her bag ready to embark on a journey that will take her from one place to the next. She believes in contentment but has found it so hard to be content.

Living in her own mind, she couldn't wait to be present with her Lord. To completely worship Him -

Her bag contained the usual makeup, the prayer beads and one Scarf.

Completely present with herself.

It took her a few hours to get to London. She was nearly ready to depart for her spiritual journey.

JANUARY

6

. . . .

Stone Soup

the little grenade
that sits gently waiting
accepting earths falls
kamikaze grace, graced by everything
A little harmonica playing
gives the chest room to escape
over a bridge, she hides away

in terrains of sun and terrains of salt
she has read all the pilgrims
and learnt about marcelled hands
told herself she was fortunate enough
to withstand the mismatch of time and place
being in her heart and yet belonging no where in her mind

sleeping on a pillow of storm
and her hollow cheeks
hold no more warmth

it was time to put it all to rest
to send the spell down the river
and in the tilt of her head
she is handed warm soup

JANUARY

7

....

Happiness And The A-Bomb

My happiness would be explosive. exploding in every corner of earth. My smile would be scattered, teeth would lay in tree houses and in the ocean. People would be able to smell the scent of joy. Coffee and warm chocolate cake.

If my happiness was an atomic bomb it would leave centuries of solitude on the soil. It would grow more and more flowers. The sun will shine and the people will rise and so lives will ache to be told.

~~FIN~~

JANUARY

8

....

Images By Listening

A bird
A group of birds trying to spread their wings
A swarming sense of white light
Gushing from windows
I couldn't quite make anything else out
I had this sense of need to escape but an overwhelming gratitude
for being here and being present
Glasses. Dark frames. A serious nature

Am I allowing myself to see
or do I have too many blocks and veils hiding my true heart

desires

A cageless freedom begins with the
excessive swarm of light
A pilgramage of warmth
finds a place to stay
Atop the canopy of the sky is an open hand
Fire brigadge saving sandless stillness
A decay of the ill temper and procrastination
The birth of something new means martyrdom
of delicate tone

JANUARY

9

. . . .

They Say It's Your Birthday

They say it's your birthday

Born out of love and warmth

They say it's your birthday

You living breathing ember

A spark of some fascination and body inclination

Someone slithered and settled

Making you a celebration

conquered civilisation

Despite birthdays and their reputation

Its your time to fall compliant

Plenty of chocolate cake

And dances from everynation

they say its your birthday

I said it was your birthday

long ago

JANUARY

10

. . . .

Alphabet Letter Of The Day

Reeling   Ready
Religion   Reverie
Relation   Righteousness
Reliability   Reality
                 Reason
Radio   Rigid
Record   Record
Rinsing
Ringing
Ring
Ripe

Reeling in this ripening ready rope
I realise my reverie has no way
of hoping itself better

The same record plays on and on
And the ringing in my ears can't hold
the sound of the radio

It's a matter of soul reliability
and I can't seem to understand
such rigid perception

The reasoning is relentlessly tiring me
And I have made a religion out of my
insecurities

It's not the same as living everyday
in castle rage
It's just a strange place

I hope my reasoning rids me of all
that isn't serving me

JANUARY

11

. . . .

Surprise City

Baghdad
Begins its jazzy blues on the streets
People congregate with their tapping feet
The laughter rises from the roadsides
like a young childs beady eyes
eating cotton candy
And pressing its lips against a rusy taxi window

the blues spread on and the men begin to

swing
young boys

JANUARY

12

....

Letter To An Artist

Dear Frida,
I have you pictured on my wall, in my notebook, I have mini art pieces
and books, mugs, lunchbags. I wonder if you ever thought you would

be iconic or whether you would have

JANUARY

13

....

Every Explorer

JANUARY

14

. . . .

Keep Running

JANUARY

15

. . . .

The Rules

JANUARY

16

· ·

Twenty Oil And Snow

JANUARY

17

....

A Life Worth Writing About

JANUARY

18

....

A Sticky Situation

JANUARY

19

. . . .

The Legend Of Poe

JANUARY

20

....

Reoccurring Words And Dreams

mercury magic makes the mood seem melancholy

A dream that persists to play

Petrified of night

day felt like an escape

we sink in our bodies and build against shapes

night strips our defences away

we weep with agony

split by a sea of healing and prayer

somehow we make it through the night

fists curled like we are ready to fight

our frames timed

unleash our clothes

healing is stripping pain

practice patience through prayer and knowing the worst is over

you decide to feel liberated again

the snow fell through the night

our lips are bleeding from cold cuts

and weepy eyes

JANUARY

21

....

Use Some Sense

My fingers cold and pointed
The tastebuds relish the tangyness
the breeze sweet on my chest
The smell of citrus
And open window breath
contagious morning scent
catches us off-guard

Breeze cuts on my face
tangy pineapple potion

....

Couplet Lost

JANUARY

23

. . . .

Titling Dali

JANUARY

24

. . . .

Twin Form

25

. . . .

I Abstractly Love Your Concreteness

JANUARY

26

. . . .

Large To Small

....

Journalistic Inspiration

# JANUARY

28

....

Splatterings And Drippings

29

. . . .

Twitter Me This

JANUARY

30

....

Overheard Poetry

JANUARY

31

. . . .

Yet Another Sticky Situation

FEBRUARY

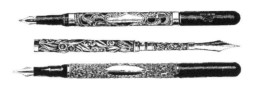

Goals/Notes/Doodles:

FEBRUARY

1

....

Langston Hughes

FEBRUARY

2

. . . .

Starting Over

FEBRUARY

3

....

Money Changes Everything

FEBRUARY

4

....

The Language Of Facebook

FEBRUARY

5

. . . .

Jokes And Laughs

FEBRUARY

6

. . . .

Integrated Circuits

FEBRUARY

7

. . . .

Laboring-Saving Devices

FEBRUARY

8

....

Under Elizabeth Bishop's Spell

FEBRUARY

9

. . . .

Incremental

FEBRUARY

10

. . . .

Get Thee To A Library

FEBRUARY

11

....

Dream Weaver

FEBRUARY

12

....

Abraham Lincoln

FEBRUARY

13

....

Synonym / Antonym

FEBRUARY

14

. . . .

Be Mine

FEBRUARY

15

....

Liar, Liar, Pants On Fire

FEBRUARY

16

. . . .

Shadow

FEBRUARY

17

. . . .

Winter

FEBRUARY

18

. . . .

Still Gray

FEBRUARY

19

. . . .

Obsolete

FEBRUARY

20

. . . .

Directions

FEBRUARY

21

....

Poem Of Address

FEBRUARY

22

. . . .

Washington's Birthday

FEBRUARY

23

. . . .

Sonnet In Four Sentences

FEBRUARY

24

....

If You Could Be Anybody

FEBRUARY

25

. . . .

Time Travel

FEBRUARY

26

....

Just Like A Prayer

FEBRUARY

27

....

Anaphora

FEBRUARY

28

. . . .

Vice

FEBRUARY

29

....

Leaping

MARCH

Goals/Notes/Doodles:

MARCH

1

....

Another Way To Be Faithful

MARCH

2

....

One Fish, Two Fish, Red Fish, Blue Fish

MARCH

3

....

Sugarbeep, I Love You

4

....

You Look Like Marilyn Monroe, Except In The Eyes

MARCH

5

....

Midnight And You're Awake

6

....

I Prefer Chocolate Chip

MARCH

7

....

Let It Break

MARCH

8

....

Where Have You Gone, Joe DiMaggio?

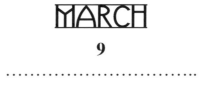

MARCH

9

....

Oh, God!

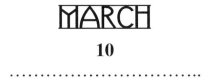

MARCH

10

....

Choose Your Own Odd Couple

MARCH

11

....

Deja Vu

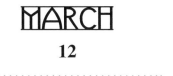

MARCH

12

....

A Guide To Life

MARCH

13

....

Wish

14

....

Sylvia Beach And Shakespeare & Co.

MARCH

15

....

Meandering To The Answer

MARCH

16

....

Periwinkle K

MARCH

17

The Luck Of The Irish

MARCH

18

....

A Poem About Nothing

MARCH

19

....

Gamble Your Life Away

MARCH

20

....

The Yoko Factor

MARCH

21

....

Save Ferris

MARCH

22

....

Many Lies And One Truth

MARCH

23

....

Starlets

MARCH

24

. . . .

The Magician's Tricks

25

. . . .

Opposite Day At Sunset

MARCH

26

....

Whitman Chocolates

MARCH

27

....

The Numbers Have It

MARCH

28

....

Underwater

MARCH

29

....

Sacred Past

MARCH

30

. . . .

Our Love's In Jeopardy

31

....

Surprise Party For Mom

APRIL

Goals/Notes/Doodles:

APRIL

1

. . . .

April Fool's

APRIL

2

. . . .

Collage

APRIL

3

....

Concrete

APRIL

4

....

Notebook

APRIL

5

....

I Remember

APRIL

6

. . . .

Skate-Away

APRIL

7

....

Backwards Acrostic

APRIL

8

....

Let's Escape

APRIL

9

....

Deprivation Vs. Plentitude

APRIL

10

....

Only Fasten

APRIL

11

....

Virtue Comes To Visit

APRIL

12

....

Blissful And Miraculous

APRIL

13

....

Digging For Dirt

APRIL

14

....

After The Rain

APRIL

15

....

Mr. Da Vinci's Art

APRIL

16

....

Return Of The Extinct Animal

APRIL

17

....

He Said / She Said

APRIL

18

....

Father Of The Beats

APRIL

19

....

Death Bed

APRIL

20

. . . .

Mother Tongue

APRIL

21

....

Your Favorite Word/s

APRIL

22

....

Earth Day

APRIL

23

. . . .

Shakespearean Sonnet

APRIL

24

....

No Ideas But In Things

APRIL

25

....

So This Is ___

APRIL

26

....

A Horse Walks Into A Bar

APRIL

27

....

Elegy

APRIL

28

. . . .

The Edible School Yard

APRIL

29

. . . .

Beautiful And Dangerous

....

What's In A Name?

MAY

Goals/Notes/Doodles:

MAY

1

....

May Day

MAY

2

....

Weather Or Not

MAY

3

....

Mysterious Life Of Washington, D.C.

MAY

4

....

Breaking The Rules

5

....

Pat, I'd Like To Buy A Vowel

MAY

6

....

Large Subject, Small Poem

Around The Corner Comes Dumb Luck

8

....

Paper Or Laptop

MAY

9

....

Metaphor Metaphor

MAY

10

....

Feels Like The First Time

MAY

11

. . . .

Psychic Poet

12

....

Back From The Past

MAY

13

....

Classical Jazz

MAY

14

....

Father Figure

MAY

15

. . . .

Emily Lives

MAY

16

....

The "You" Poem

....

Index Card Fun

MAY

18

....

I Don't Know Where I'm Gonna Go When The Volcano Blows

MAY

19

....

A Pair Of Couplets

MAY

20

. . . .

Rosanna Rosanna Danna

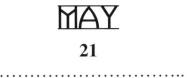

MAY

21

. . . .

Langston's Titles

MAY

22

. . . .

Mysteries Inside

MAY

23

....

Library Field Trip

....

What's In The Pantry

MAY

25

. . . .

Taboo You

MAY

26

....

A–Z

MAY

27

....

Contrary Day

MAY

28

. . . .

Bridging The Gap

MAY

29

....

Hope, Thanks, And Memories

30

....

Mixed Travel Plans

MAY

31

....

Big Ben

JUNE

Goals/Notes/Doodles:

JUNE

1

....

Lovely Rita Meter Maid

JUNE

2

....

Curse

JUNE

3

. . . .

Country Of Origin

JUNE

4

....

The Right To Vote

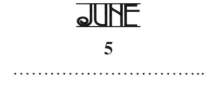

JUNE

5

. . . .

Field Guide To The Animals

JUNE

6

....

D-Day

JUNE

7

. . . .

Who Are You?

`

JUNE

8

....

Decade, Decade On The Wall

JUNE

9

....

Rock Star

JUNE

10

....

Spam It Up

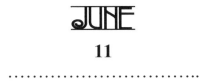

JUNE

11

....

Found

JUNE

12

....

Statue Of Elvis Found On Mars

JUNE

13

....

Inaugural Poem

JUNE

14

....

Flag Day

JUNE

15

. . . .

Talking Visual Art

JUNE

16

....

The Good, The Bad, And The Ugly

17

....

American Sentences

JUNE

18

....

Experiments With Reading

JUNE

19

. . . .

Scaffolding

20

. . . .

Giving Back

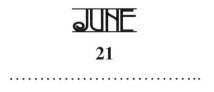

JUNE

21

....

Solstice

JUNE

22

. . . .

Year Of Your Birth

JUNE

23

. . . .

Self-Taught

JUNE

24

....

Opposites

JUNE

25

. . . .

One Degree Of Separation

JUNE

26

....

The Story Of Words

JUNE

27

. . . .

Blessing

JUNE

28

. . . .

Road Trip

29

....

Hate

JUNE

1

....

What Will You Tell The Aliens?

JULY

Goals/Notes/Doodles:

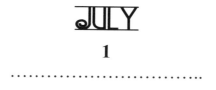

JULY

1

....

Poem Of Place

JULY

2

. . . .

Apology

JULY

3

....

What's Your Cultural Identity

JULY

4

....

Fourth Of July

JULY

5

....

Don Your Dali Moustache Day

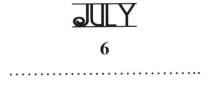

JULY

6

. . . .

Winter In July

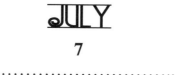

JULY

7

. . . .

How To Cook A Wolf

JULY

8

....

Good Humor Ice Cream Truck

JULY

9

....

Phobias

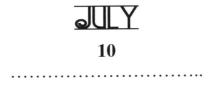

10

. . . .

Search-Engines

JULY

11

. . . .

She Blinded Me With Science

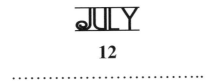

JULY

12

....

Channeling Neruda's Wildness

....

Burden Basket

JULY

14

. . . .

Burrowing

JULY

15

....

One-Rhyme Poem

JULY

16

....

What's Funny About A Headstone

17

. . . .

Meeting The Parents

18

....

Get A Job

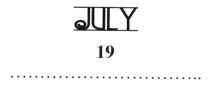

JULY

19

....

On Your List

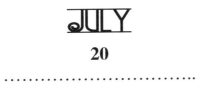

JULY

20

. . . .

Coined Words

JULY

21

....

Here's The Report

JULY

22

....

We'll Be Driving

JULY
23

....

Find A Museum

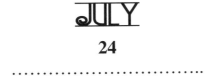

JULY

24

. . . .

Why I Hate The Color Blue

....

Swearing Off

JULY

26

....

Portrait

JULY

27

....

Grateful / Dread

JULY

28

. . . .

Pantoum

....

New Knowledge

JULY
30

. . . .

Death

JULY

31

....

Gritty, Gutsy, And Groveling

AUGUST

Goals/Notes/Doodles:

 AUGUST

1

....

Juxtapose Life

AUGUST

2

. . . .

Acrostic Place

AUGUST

3

....

In The Surreal World

AUGUST

4

....

I Want A New Drug

. . . .

Words Inside Words

AUGUST

6

. . . .

Atomic Memories

AUGUST

7

....

Make It Happen

....

What's Up, Doc?

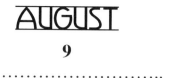

AUGUST

9

. . . .

City Nature

AUGUST

10

. . . .

In Six

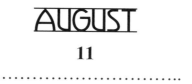

AUGUST

11

....

Headliners

AUGUST

12

. . . .

Meteor Middle

AUGUST

13

. . . .

Sharpshooters

AUGUST

14

. . . .

Dog Days

AUGUST

15

· ·

Woodstock Inspiration

AUGUST

16

. . . .

The History Of Names

....

A Quote Can Start A Thousand Poems

AUGUST

18

. . . .

Where You Are Now

AUGUST

19

. . . .

Linked Haiku

AUGUST

20

. . . .

Dream Syllables

AUGUST
21
....

Hawaii Without The Trees And Water

AUGUST

22

. . . .

Coloring Outside The Lines

AUGUST

23

....

Nature's Gift

24

....

Things They Never Did

AUGUST

25

. . . .

Odd Listings

AUGUST

26

....

Bad Day

....

Secrets For Friends

AUGUST

28

. . . .

Taking Dictation From The Dead

AUGUST

29

....

Times 29

AUGUST

30

....

Highway Life

AUGUST

31

....

Summer's End

SEPTEMBER

Goals/Notes/Doodles:

SEPTEMBER

1

. . . .

Bus Station, Train Station, Airport

SEPTEMBER

2

. . . .

Witness To Racism

SEPTEMBER

3

. . . .

No Life On Mars

SEPTEMBER

4

. . . .

Kodak Moment

SEPTEMBER

1

. . . .

Ecopoetics

SEPTEMBER

6

. . . .

The Future Of Poetry

SEPTEMBER

7

....

Aubade

SEPTEMBER

8

. . . .

Temper, Temper!

SEPTEMBER

9

· ·

I Come From

SEPTEMBER

10

....

You Do Not Have To Be Good

SEPTEMBER

11

. . . .

9/11

SEPTEMBER

12

. . . .

You're Not Going To Believe This, But

SEPTEMBER

13

. . . .

Poking Fun At Metaphor

SEPTEMBER

14

. . . .

How The Pope Gets Chosen

SEPTEMBER

15

....

But I Digress

SEPTEMBER

16

....

I Don't Like It

SEPTEMBER

17

. . . .

The Happy Genius Of My Household

SEPTEMBER

18

. . . .

Water, Water Everywhere

SEPTEMBER

19

. . . .

Sweep Away The Scaffolding

SEPTEMBER

20

....

The Things

SEPTEMBER

21

....

Cleaning Out The Gecko Cage

SEPTEMBER

22

. . . .

First Word, Same Word

SEPTEMBER

23

. . . .

Bless You

SEPTEMBER

24

....

I've Looked At Clouds

SEPTEMBER

25

. . . .

Nonsense

SEPTEMBER

26

....

T.S. Eliot

SEPTEMBER

27

....

Migration

SEPTEMBER

28

. . . .

Jargon Talking

SEPTEMBER

29

. . . .

Cliché Mash-Up

SEPTEMBER

30

. . . .

O Pile Of White Shirts

OCTOBER

Goals/Notes/Doodles:

OCTOBER

1

. . . .

The Full Moon

OCTOBER

2

. . . .

The Beginning Of The Fall

OCTOBER

3

....

The Marriage

OCTOBER

4

....

Sputnik!

OCTOBER

5

. . . .

Breakfast At Your House

OCTOBER

6

....

Pop-Art In An American Supermarket

OCTOBER

7

....

Nevermore

OCTOBER

8

....

A Small Event Began It

OCTOBER

9

....

Imagine

 OCTOBER

10

. . . .

Tuxedo City

OCTOBER

11

....

SNL Through The Years

OCTOBER

12

....

Picnic In The Wrong Season

OCTOBER

13

. . . .

Who's Afraid Of Any Author?

OCTOBER

14

. . . .

Interruptions Please

OCTOBER

15

....

I Do Love Lucy

OCTOBER

16

. . . .

Ever Been To Paris?

OCTOBER

17

....

Money Matters

OCTOBER

18

....

Telephone Game

OCTOBER

19

. . . .

The Fake Version Of Your Life

OCTOBER

20

....

100 Words On Dewey

OCTOBER

21

. . . .

I'm So Dizzy

OCTOBER

22

....

Over-Punctuate Me

OCTOBER

23

....

Late Night TV

OCTOBER

24

....

What Falls

OCTOBER

25

....

Picasso It

OCTOBER

26

. . . .

Holiday Upon Holiday

OCTOBER

27

....

Ms. Plath And Her Fruit

OCTOBER

28

....

Leaves

OCTOBER

29

. . . .

Superstitious

OCTOBER

30

. . . .

Spooky

OCTOBER

31

....

All Hallow's Eve

NOVEMBER

Goals/Notes/Doodles:

NOVEMBER

1

....

All Saints' Day

2

....

Leftover Candy

NOVEMBER

3

....

What's The Weather Out There?

4

. . . .

Weddings "R" Us

NOVEMBER

5

. . . .

Three-Ring Circus

NOVEMBER

6

. . . .

Find A Book, Any Book

NOVEMBER

7

. . . .

Reduce / Reuse / Recycle

NOVEMBER

8

. . . .

Dear Constellation

....

Holy Poetry-Writing, Batman

10

....

Sesame Street And Muppet Man

NOVEMBER

11

....

Veterans Day

NOVEMBER

12

. . . .

Found On The Page

13

. . . .

.

What You Wanted To Say

NOVEMBER

14

. . . .

Teach Us

NOVEMBER

15

....

Ms. O'Keeffe's Larger Than Life Flowers

NOVEMBER

16

....

Mini Abecedarian Poem

NOVEMBER

17

....

Your Own Bookstore

NOVEMBER

18

. . . .

Sounds And How They Repeat

NOVEMBER

19

. . . .

Multisyllabic Words And The Compassion They Show

NOVEMBER

20

. . . .

Small Talk

NOVEMBER

21

. . . .

No Good Stories Come From "After We Ate A Salad"

NOVEMBER

22

. . . .

Second Person, This One's For You

NOVEMBER

23

. . . .

That's A Negative

NOVEMBER

24

....

Old Flame

NOVEMBER

25

....

Dear Fill-In-The-Blank

26

. . . .

But At Least There Was Pumpkin Pie

27

....

She Gives Me Love, Crazy Love

NOVEMBER

28

....

Geography

NOVEMBER

29

....

First Words

30

....

Mark Twain And Tom Sawyer

DECEMBER

Goals/Notes/Doodles:

DECEMBER

1

. . . .

Scrabble

DECEMBER

2

. . . .

Chanukah

DECEMBER

3

. . . .

Cosmic

DECEMBER

4

....

You Must Change Your Life

DECEMBER

5

. . . .

Glosa

DECEMBER

6

....

Hip Haiku

DECEMBER

7

. . . .

To-Do List

DECEMBER

8

. . . .

Letter To An Abstract Noun

. . . .

Help Me Rondeau

DECEMBER

10

. . . .

Fame Is A Fickle Food

DECEMBER

11

. . . .

Shoe Poem

DECEMBER

12

....

When Wisdom Knocks

DECEMBER

13

....

James Wright

DECEMBER

14

. . . .

Carnival

DECEMBER

15

....

No More Masks!

DECEMBER

16

....

Mall Visit

DECEMBER

17

....

What Would Mr. Brady Say?

DECEMBER

18

....

The Receptionist

DECEMBER

19

....

This I Believe

DECEMBER

20

....

Tell Me What You Want

DECEMBER
21

....

Darkness

DECEMBER

22

. . . .

In Praise Of The Return Of Light

DECEMBER

23

. . . .

Robert Bly

DECEMBER

24

. . . .

In The Beginning

DECEMBER

25

. . . .

Haiku For Three

DECEMBER

26

. . . .

Universe

DECEMBER

27

. . . .

Hey, Mr. Spaceman

DECEMBER

28

. . . .

Favorite Childhood Food

DECEMBER

29

....

Palm Poem

DECEMBER

30

. . . .

Ingredients List

DECEMBER

31

. . . .

Making Light Of Taking Stock

Publications by Two Sylvias Press:

The Daily Poet: Day-By-Day Prompts For Your Writing Practice
by Kelli Russell Agodon and Martha Silano (Print and eBook)

The Daily Poet Companion Journal (Print)

Fire On Her Tongue: An Anthology of Contemporary Women's Poetry
edited by Kelli Russell Agodon and Annette Spaulding-Convy (Print and eBook)

The Poet Tarot and Guidebook: A Deck Of Creative Exploration (Print)

What The Truth Tastes Like
by Martha Silano (Print and eBook)

landscape / heartbreak
by Michelle Peñaloza (Print and eBook)

Earth, Winner of the 2014 Two Sylvias Press Chapbook Prize
by Cecilia Woloch (Print and eBook)

The Cardiologist's Daughter
by Natasha Kochicheril Moni (Print and eBook)

She Returns to the Floating World
by Jeannine Hall Gailey (Print and eBook)

Hourglass Museum
by Kelli Russell Agodon (eBook)

Cloud Pharmacy
by Susan Rich (eBook)

Dear Alzheimer's: A Caregiver's Diary & Poems
by Esther Altshul Helfgott (eBook)

Listening to Mozart: Poems of Alzheimer's
by Esther Altshul Helfgott (eBook)

Crab Creek Review 30th Anniversary Issue featuring Northwest Poets
edited by Kelli Russell Agodon and Annette Spaulding-Convy (eBook)

Please visit Two Sylvias Press (www.twosylviaspress.com) for information on purchasing our print books, eBooks, writing tools, and for submission guidelines for our annual chapbook prize. Two Sylvias Press also offers editing services and manuscript consultations.

Created with the belief that great writing
is good for the world.

two sylvias press

Visit us online: www.twosylviaspress.com

Printed in Great Britain
by Amazon

34543342R00232